☑ **Y0-DOK-374**

In my Opinion...

Compiled by Gary Poole
Illustrated by Don Orehek

tempo
books

GROSSET & DUNLAP
A Filmways Company
Publishers • New York

In My Opinion . . .

ISBN: 0-448-17168-6

A Tempo Books Original
Printed in the United States of America
Published simultaneously in Canada

Contents

Introduction

TIRED OF BEING TOLD WHAT TO LIKE?
      NOW YOU CAN:

    (1) WRITE YOUR OWN REVIEWS!
    (2) MAKE YOUR OWN LISTS!
    (3) EXPRESS YOUR OWN OPINIONS!

STRIKE A BLOW FOR INDIVIDUALITY!

TELL IT LIKE IT IS!

CHAPTER ONE

ME, MYSELF AND I
(An honest look!)

REVIEW OF MYSELF
(Fill in the blanks.)

My name is _Monica_ and I am a
nice person!
When people get to know me, the first thing they
notice is my _smile_ and my _ex_____ !
I have _____ and _____ .
I tend to be modest about my _____
and my _____ and I especially don't like
to brag about my _____, even though
I have the _____ in the world and
can _____ better than anybody!
I like to _____ with my friends and
play _____ and _____ .
When we get together it's absolutely _____and
_____ !
I am _____, _____, and _____ .
I like to feel that I'm _____ !
All in all, I think I'm _____
and the _____ .

2

MY DIET

My favorite foods are: _Fruits_,
breads, _vedgedbals_
_____, _Meats breads_,
and _Milk_.

I try to eat healthy foods, like _Fruits_
meats, and _breads_.

I try to avoid _candies_
chips _gum_
_____.

My weight right now is _75_. I would like to
weigh _65_.

There is an old saying, "You are what you eat."
If that is true, then I want to be a _Nurse_
and not a _Singer_!

Breakfast is _a good_ meal
of the day, because it "breaks" the "fast." A good
breakfast should contain _Meat_, _Milk_,
bread, and _Fruits_.

As far as diet goes, I plan to _eat_
properly _every_
singal _day_.

ACTIVITIES

I like to _____, _____ , and
_____ . Sometimes _____ can
be fun, but my favorite activity is _____ !

COMMENTS

5

PHYSICAL FITNESS

Exercise is _____
_____ .
To keep fit I _____ ,
_____ , _____ ,
and _____ .
Sports I engage in are _____ ,
_____ , _____ ,
and _____ .
I can do _____ push-ups.
I can do _____ sit-ups.
I can do _____ jumping jacks.
I can also _____
and _____
_____ .
I believe in physical fitness and plan to _____
_____
_____
_____ .

MY MOODS

Like all people, I have many moods. Sometimes I'm _____ .

Sometimes I feel like _____
_____
_____ .

When I feel blue, I find the best thing to do is _____
_____
_____ .

When my mood is good, I want to share it with everybody and I _____
_____
_____ .

Moods can be changed by _____
_____
_____ .

Moods are important. They show we are human and have feelings. It is also important to be considerate of other people's moods, too. So when I sense that someone is feeling _____, I always try to _____ .

MY PHILOSOPHY ON LIFE

I think life is _____
_____
_____
_____.

I think people should _____
_____
_____.

It would be a great world if _____
_____
_____
_____.

I try to greet each day with _____
_____.

I want to live my life so that _____
_____.

In the future, I hope to _____
_____
_____.

Whatever happens, I will always _____
_____
_____.

I am going to try to be _____, _____
_____, and _____.
That is my philosophy. Those are my feelings.

_____

MONTHLY SUMMARY

JANUARY _____
_____
_____

FEBRUARY _____
_____
_____

MARCH _____
_____
_____

APRIL _____
_____
_____

MAY _____
_____
_____

JUNE _____
_____
_____

JULY _____

_____

_____

AUGUST _____

_____

_____

SEPTEMBER _____

_____

_____

OCTOBER _____

_____

_____

NOVEMBER _____

_____

_____

DECEMBER _____

_____

_____

CHAPTER TWO

FAMILY AND FRIENDS

MY MOTHER

My mother is _____.
Her name is _____. She is _____ tall
and has _____ hair. Her eyes are _____.
She is ____ talented. She can _____, _____,
and _____. Some days she _____
_____ and other days she _____
_____. Together we _____
_____, and _____.
She often takes me _____ and _____
_____. When I am naughty she _____
_____ and _____.
When I am good she _____ and _____.
So I try to be good all the time!

MY FATHER

My father is _____.
His name is _____. He is a _____man
and weighs _____ pounds. He is _____feet
tall. He has _____ hair and his eyes are _____.
He _____ his job. He is a _____
and he spends many hours _____.
After work, he _____ and _____
and _____. He takes me to _____
and _____ and _____.
If I misbehave he _____.
If I have a problem, he _____
_____. His favorite sport is _____
_____. He also likes _____ and _____
and _____. We share many _____
together. My father is more than a father. He is a
_____ and a good friend.

15

MY OLDER BROTHER

My older brother is _____.
His name is _____. I often go to him
for _____. He never fails to _____
and is always willing to _____.
Sometimes he doesn't want to _____,
but usually, he will _____.
He is interested in _____ and _____.
He plays _____ and _____.
He likes _____, _____, and
_____. His favorite sport is _____.
Sometimes we _____together.
He is a _____most of the time. He often tells
me _____. I listen to what
he has to say, because _____. My
older brother is _____ when it comes to __
_____ and _____. Everyone
should have an older brother who _____
_____ as well as mine does!

REVIEW OF MY YOUNGER BROTHER

_____ is my brother and he is _____
_____! I often think that I have
been _____ to have a brother that _____
_____ like he does.

Sometimes I look at him and wonder _____
_____ and _____!

He always _____and never fails
to show me _____.
When he displays that _____
I get embarrassed and don't know how to ____it.

Sometimes he _____on
me and I get _____.

My parents aren't aware of his _____
_____and I
have tried to _____but
they won't listen, because they think I'm _____
when he is the one who is _____!

Honestly, the way he gets away with _____
is absolutely _____!

17

MY YOUNGER SISTER

I can't begin to tell you how _____
it is to have a sister like _____!
She is _____ all the time!
If she's not being _____, she's being
_____. What's
more, she always _____ when I
want to _____!

Sometimes I could _____ her, but
other times I could _____ her!

When she acts _____ I get
embarrassed. Sometimes, when she _____ and
_____ I have to leave the
room.

When she puts her _____ in her
_____ and _____ her _____,
she's a real panic!

I hate it when she _____ while watching
television. I also don't like it when she _____
_____. But when she _____
_____, I just
love her for it!

All in all she's a _____ sister and I
wouldn't _____ her for _____
in the world!

18

MY OLDER SISTER

Everyone should have a sister like _____!
She likes to _____, _____,
and _____. We often _____
together. She takes me to _____, _____,
and _____. When I need advice, she is
always ready with _____.
She tells me _____, _____, and
_____. Her favorite movie star is _____
and she also likes _____. I like to
watch her _____. In her own way, she is
very _____. She is also _____,
_____, and _____.
When "push comes to shove," she is always ____
_____ and _____. I want her to know how
I feel and I think she is just _____!

MY GRANDFATHER

(Daddy's side)

Grandfather _____ is _____!
Whenever he comes to visit, he always _____
_____ and _____!
Sometimes he _____ before he even gets into
the house. He makes us _____ with
his _____.

I love the way his _____ and his
_____! When he _____
_____ and _____,
he's a scream!

Daddy says it's _____ but the
kids love it when he _____
_____. His _____
laugh is _____ and makes us all _____
_____!

I can't wait until next time when he _____
and _____! I _____ grandfather ___.
He is so _____ and

_____.

MY GRANDFATHER

(Mother's side)

Whenever grandfather _____
I get _____! He is so _____.
He _____, _____, and _____.
He makes me laugh when he _____
and _____. His face is _____
and when he smiles, the whole world just _____
_____! I always enjoy _____and
when he _____.
He makes me feel like _____.
He is always giving me _____, _____,
and _____. When Mom says no he says
_____. Of course, we don't tell
Mom that! I _____ grandfather _____.
He brings _____, and _____
into my life.

MY GRANDMOTHER

(Mother's side)

Grandmother _____ is a
real _____! Whenever I see
her, I want to _____.
She always _____
and _____ whenever
she _____.

She likes to _____ and _____
_____ and _____.

My friends call her _____.
She thinks they are _____ and _____
_____ and gets along pretty _____
with all of them.

It is something else when she _____ me
and makes _____ and _____ for
me. She is an excellent cook and makes the best
_____ you ever tasted! She also makes
_____, _____, and _____!

She tells _____ stories and makes us laugh
when she _____ and _____!

I _____ grandmother _____.
She is so _____,
and _____,

22

MY GRANDMOTHER

(Daddy's side)

Grandmother _____is a
_____. She
_____ and _____
and _____!
That's pretty good for someone who is ___years
old. It makes sense because she has been ___
_____
all her life!

She's so active she _____ and _____
every day. Of course, she can't _____as
much as she used to, but she _____instead
and makes the most out of it.

She belongs to the _____.
She attends _____every week. And
she does _____every day.

I love to listen to her _____
and watch her laugh as she _____.

She _____ a car, plays _____
and _____, and loves to _____
_____with the children. She's
_____
and great fun to have around!

MY DOG

My dog's name is _____.
The colors of _____'s coat are _____
_____.
(He/she) is a _____, and is _____
years old. _____can do tricks. (He/she)
can _____, _____, and
_____.
  We love to _____and
_____ together.
_____ is housebroken, but sometimes ____
_____. When
that happens, I have to _____!
_____'s favorite toy is _____.
(He/she) also likes to play with _____.
  _____'s favorite kinds of food are _____
and _____. Sometimes I give out_____
_____, but these are only snacks to be eaten
AFTER dinner!
  _____ is a _____dog.
Whenever people come to visit, ____is always
there to _____them!
Sometimes _____up on them
and romps with their _____.
  All in all, _____ is a _____
dog, and I wish _____
_____, because (he's/she's)
some kind of special dog!

24

MY CAT

I have a _____ cat. (His/her) name is _____. Cats are very independent, but _____ is very _____ and _____.

Whenever I _____, my cat always _____ and _____.

I like to _____ on my lap and listen to the sound of _____. _____'s tongue is very rough and it _____ whenever _____ my hand.

(He/she) likes to play _____ and will chase a _____ when I throw it across the floor.

_____'s favorite kinds of food are _____ and _____. (He/she) also likes _____. _____ is warm and _____. Sometimes, as a treat, I place a bowl of _____ on the floor for _____. When (he/she) finishes eating _____ will thank me by _____ and _____.

Cats can be real friends, and _____ is one of my closest pals.

MY BIRD

I have _____ bird(s). (His/her/their) name(s) are
_____. Birds are fun to watch.
Whenever I come over to the cage, _____ begins
to fly excitedly around. _____ is a _____
bird. It is my favorite breed.

Once _____ got out of the cage, and _____
_____, but we soon got (him/her) back inside.
The colors of my bird are _____, _____, and
_____. Since birds like to sing, _____
spends a lot of time doing just that. When a bird
sings it means they are _____.

My mother thinks the bird's singing is _____.
My brother thinks it is _____. My daddy
thinks it is _____. But I think it is _____!

To keep a bird quiet, you simply put a cover over
its cage. They think it is nighttime and _____
_____.

I always give my bird plenty of _____ and
_____. Birds love to eat and _____
is no exception. If you are careful, you can feed him
from your _____.

Birds are good company, and are easy to take
care of. They are so _____! I hope I always
have a bird.

MY FISH

Fish are fun. I don't have names for all of them, but some I do. The _____ is named _____. The _____ is named _____. And the _____ is named _____.

Fish don't seem to do much, except swim around in their tank. If you watch them carefully, you can see that they are quite playful. Sometimes they _____ and _____each other around the tank.

Other times they seem to be simply looking for _____. I love the way they _____and _____.

There's one fish in particular that _____ _____. He is my special fish. His colors are _____, _____, and _____. He is a _____.

I have to be careful not to _____or else they will get _____. I try to keep their _____ clean, so they will stay healthy.

All in all, fish are pretty and they are good _____.

MY OTHER PET

I have a _____. It's a(n)
_____ sort of a pet, but I
love it. Whenever I want to _____it's
always there to _____me.

I love it when it _____
and my _____! It makes my life so _____
_____!

When I come home my _____is always
_____ on the floor. So I reach down and
pick up _____ and toss _____
_____ into the air. Sometimes, instead of ___
it, I _____ it and _____in bed
with me.

Playful as _____, it can _____
and _____ until all hours!

When the _____ gets _____
I have to _____. And if that's not enough,
I will _____with it.

I wouldn't trade my _____for all the
_____ in the world!

MY BEST FRIEND

(Male)

I have many friends, but _____
is my best friend! I met him at _____
_____. We hit it off right from the start.
He likes _____, _____, and
_____, and so do I!

We often go _____together.
Other times we'll _____, _____,
or _____.

We even have fun if we just _____
around the house!

If I have a problem, I can _____
_____ and _____will
listen and _____.
He knows I would _____for him, too!

He is like a brother to me, only he's _____
_____and I can tell him things I wouldn't tell
_____.

Sometimes we share each other's _____
and _____. It's great to have a friend
to share things with, and _____.

Having someone you can count on is _____
_____ and _____is
always there when I _____.

MY BEST FRIEND

(Female)

My best friend is _____.
We always have _____when
we are together. We _____, _____,
and _____ a lot!

Some people think we are being silly, but actually we are _____.

I first met _____ at _____
_____. It took awhile, but after we got to know
each other we _____.

So we became friends and _____
_____.

We often go _____together.
Sometimes we _____, _____
_____, and _____.
_____ likes to _____.
She also likes _____, _____,
and _____.

It's great to have a pal like _____.
We both share the same interests and _____.
We always look forward to _____
_____, and
try to get together as much as possible!

31

MY FAVORITE TEACHER

(Female)

My favorite teacher is Ms. _____.
She is _____, _____, and _____!
I also like her because _____
_____.

Her classroom is always_____.
The kids can _____
_____, but Ms. _____
keeps a sharp eye on _____
at all times.

She always has time for _____
and _____. Whenever
I am _____she tells me to
_____.

She is very fair. If I'm unable to _____,
she will _____ until I _____
_____.

She wears _____ and _____.
Her hair is _____. She has a good sense of
_____, and her laugh is _____.

When we are _____she can get very
_____! That's when we have to _____
and I don't mean maybe!

I will hate to move up from Ms. ____'s class.
Poor thing! She's been in the __grade for years!

MY FAVORITE TEACHER

(Male)

My favorite teacher is Mr. _____.
He _____
_____whenever the
opportunity arises. He never fails to _____
me when I'm _____ or _____
me when I'm _____!

His classroom is _____from the moment we
enter it! He is very _____of
all his pupils, and spends a lot of _____
_____.

He gives us a lot of _____to do, but
we don't mind, because he also gives us fun things
to
_____!

When the going gets rough, _____gets
_____! Then he gets _____
and we have to _____or else
he'll _____!

When I graduate from Mr. _____'s class, I
will be _____. I will think back over
this year as one of the _____!

If I become _____later in life
and _____, I will owe
it all to Mr. _____!

MY NEIGHBORHOOD

I live in a _____ neighborhood.
The people who live here are _____, ____,
and _____. There are some _____
living on the next block and we _____
very well when we _____ together.
   Occasionally, there's a _____
in the streets, but otherwise, it's just a(n) _____
_____ neighborhood with lots of _____
_____ going on all the time.
   The buildings here are _____
_____. Our home is
_____. It can get _____
_____ at times, but then we just _____
and _____ and the living is easy!
   Sometimes I wish _____
_____, but then I look around and feel ____
_____. So it's all a matter of _____
_____ and how you _____!
   If you can _____ and _____, you've got
it made around here!

MY BOYFRIEND

I guess you could say that _____
is my boyfriend. Boyfriends are different from best
friends because _____
_____.
Anyway, I feel different when I am around ___.
I feel _____, _____, and _____!
Sometimes I just don't know what to _____
when I am with him.
He is very _____, _____, and
_____ when he is with me. He doesn't try to
show off or _____
_____.
So, I guess that means he _____about me.
We have gone _____together. Also
we have _____, _____, and
_____.
We think going steady is _____.
So we plan to _____until we get older.
Right now, he's my "boy" friend, with "quotes"
around it. Which means, "sort of."
I am sure there will be lots of boys who will
interest me, but _____is someone very special!

MY GIRLFRIEND

I like to think of _____
as my girlfriend. She has as much as said she is,
although she dates _____
_____ and _____!
That is, if you can call _____dating!
I honestly don't see how she can be attracted to
_____ and me at the same time.
We're complete _____.

So, whenever I'm with her, I try to be _____
_____.
I figure if I'm _____, she will _____
and that will set me apart from _____
_____!

We have gone _____together.
Also we have _____, _____,
and _____. I really do enjoy
her company.

She is _____, _____, and
_____. Sometimes she's _____, and
that drives me up the walls!

When I point out her _____, she gets very
_____ and tells me _____.

I like _____very, very much. And I
think she _____about me.

MY EX-BOYFRIEND

_____ is my ex-boyfriend because _____
_____
_____
_____
_____!

He is _____, _____, and
_____!

If I had a _____ I would wish her a _____ like _____!

Every time I think of him, I _____
_____.

When he _____
_____, that's when I knew it was all over!

We can remain "just friends" and I wish him all the _____ in the world!

MY EX-GIRLFRIEND

Going with ＿＿＿＿＿＿＿＿＿＿＿＿was like ＿＿＿＿＿＿＿＿＿＿＿＿＿＿＿＿＿
＿＿＿＿＿＿＿＿＿＿＿＿＿＿＿＿＿！
I spent ＿＿＿＿＿＿＿＿with that girl, and I know what I'm talking about. I didn't mind it when she ＿＿＿＿＿＿＿＿ and ＿＿＿＿＿＿
＿＿＿＿＿＿＿＿＿, but when she ＿＿＿＿
＿＿＿＿＿＿＿＿＿ and ＿＿＿＿＿＿＿＿＿, well, that was ＿＿＿＿＿＿＿＿＿＿＿＿！
She's a nice girl, but ＿＿＿＿＿＿＿＿＿
＿＿＿＿＿＿＿＿＿＿＿＿＿＿＿＿＿＿＿.
I'm sure she means well when she ＿＿＿＿
＿＿＿＿＿＿＿＿＿＿＿＿＿＿＿＿＿＿＿
and ＿＿＿＿＿＿＿＿＿＿＿！
It's all a matter of personal taste, so when she ＿＿＿＿＿＿ and ＿＿＿＿＿＿＿, and ＿＿＿＿
＿＿＿＿＿＿＿＿, that's okay by me.
She likes to ＿＿＿＿＿＿, ＿＿＿＿＿＿＿, and ＿＿＿＿＿＿. While I like to ＿＿＿＿＿＿,
＿＿＿＿＿＿＿, and ＿＿＿＿＿＿＿＿
＿＿＿＿＿＿＿＿＿.
We're just different, I guess. They say "opposites attract," but in our case, they ＿＿＿＿
＿＿＿＿＿＿＿＿＿＿＿＿＿＿＿＿＿＿＿.
I hope she finds a boyfriend who ＿＿＿＿＿
＿＿＿＿＿＿＿＿＿＿＿＿＿＿＿＿＿＿＿.
I wish them both well.

CHAPTER THREE

THE ARTS

TELEVISION REVIEW

Watching television is like _____
_____. When something good
comes on, you _____! Last night's
premiere of _____ was _____.
If you ever wanted to _____you
could have seen it last night. It was pure_____
from the word go.

The idea behind this _____is
_____. The actors are _____
and the script they have to work with is _____.
_____has the lead, and she does
_____ with _____.

Her co-star _____seems
_____ in the role. The two of them
together _____very well. However,
when it comes to _____, they _____!

Whoever dreamed up this _____should
be _____! If this gets nominated for an
Emmy, you can be sure it _____.

Watch for it next week if you want to _____
_____! Once again television has brought us _
_____ and we should _____.

TELEVISION REVIEW

Well, if ever there was _____
on television, last night's showing of _____
_____was a prime example.

The setting is _____during the
_____. While the costumes seemed
authentic enough for that period, the fact that they
had _____automobiles to ride around in seemed
ridiculous, to say the least.

The writing was _____. This
may be the producer's fault, because it seems
obvious that the writers were given freedom to
distort history at will and _____
_____!

As far as the acting goes, the _____said
the better! It was _____
_____.

The only performer who stood out was _____
_____. He _____
_____.
And that's not bad for a dog who only had a walk-
on!

If the networks continue to program "specials"
like these, I only hope they will _____
_____.

MY OWN TELEVISION REVIEW

_____
_____
_____
_____
_____
_____
_____
_____
_____
_____
_____
_____
_____
_____
_____
_____
_____
_____
_____
_____

MOVIE REVIEW

"_____" is the
kind of movie you'd take your _____
to see. It is _____
_____.
_____ and _____
_____ are the stars and they _____
_____,
_____ is completely _____
in the role of _____, the man
who _____
_____.
   As _____, the woman who _____
_____,
I thought _____was absolutely
_____ in her
intepretation of the role.
   The photography was _____
_____.
The scenery was _____.
However, I felt that _____
was spent on _____, and tended
to _____ the story down.
   If you like _____and
_____, then
"_____" would
be just your cup of tea.

42

MOVIE REVIEW

Sitting through "_____"
is like _____.
It is a _____experience.
   You are asked to believe that _____
_____.
If you can go along with that, then you can ____
_____,
because the rest of the film is _____
_____.
   I must say, I _____when
the _____
_____.
   What I didn't like was _____
_____
_____.
   Aside from that, I thought the picture as a whole
was _____, _____, and _____.
   I don't often recommend _____films, but
if you can _____
_____,
you might get a kick out of this one!
   By the way, _____was his usual self
in the lead role, and so was _____
as his _____ co-star.

43

MY OWN MOVIE REVIEW

_____
_____
_____
_____
_____
_____
_____
_____
_____
_____
_____
_____
_____
_____
_____
_____
_____
_____
_____

BOOK REVIEW

"_____"

(Title)

Occasionally a book comes along that _____
_____. The author _____
_____ seems to _____when he takes
pen in hand. His _____of the English
language is _____. He writes
on _____levels, so that the reader can
_____, if he desires.

The plot is _____drawn, with many
_____ along the way. The reader is _____
and led in _____ direction and then _____
and _____! By twists and turns the clever
_____ take hold and _____the
imagination.

The characterizations are _____.
Each one is clear as _____. The heroine is
so _____ you feel like _____her right
from the start. To put yourself in the hero's ____
is a natural reaction.

Never has so much _____ and _____
come our way. If you read this book you are bound
to _____ and _____!

MY OWN BOOK REVIEW

_____
_____
_____
_____
_____
_____
_____
_____
_____
_____
_____
_____
_____
_____
_____
_____
_____
_____
_____

MY FAVORITE ACTOR

My favorite actor is _____.
When his face comes on the screen, I _____
_____!
He is so _____!
He can _____, _____,
and _____.
When he _____, I just go
bananas! And when he _____, well, that's
too much!
I saw him recently in "_____,"
and what he did with that role was _____
_____.
He is more than just a(n) _____
_____. As a serious actor he ranks _____
_____, and can _____
with the best of them!
I have been a fan of his since _____when I
saw him in " _____,"
and I have been following his career ever since.
If he ever appears around here in person, I
certainly plan to _____.
_____, you're the greatest!

MY FAVORITE ACTRESS

My favorite actress is _____.
I think she is _____
because she _____
_____.
  When I saw her act in " _____ "
I thought she was _____.
She took a part that was _____
_____ and turned it into _____
_____.
  She is capable of _____.
She can _____, _____, and
_____.
  I love the way she _____
_____.
  Her figure is _____ and her hair is _____
_____. Her face is _____.
  She can play any part _____, _____,
or _____! It doesn't matter what she does.
Even if the story is weak, she manages to _____
_____and make it interesting.
  So three cheers for _____!
She's the best, and I'm her No. 1 _____!

MY FAVORITE COMEDIENNE

I first saw _____ on
_____, and since then
she has been my favorite comedienne. She has
got to be one of the funniest females of all time—if
not THE funniest!

When she _____
_____ and _____
_____,
she has me in stitches!

Even though she can make her face look ___,
_____, or _____, she still keeps
her natural beauty. When she isn't clowning, she's
a very _____ woman.

I also think she is _____. She is
no dummy, that's for sure, and knows _____
_____.

As an actress, she is _____,
and I am certain she could handle a _____
part if she were ever offered one.

I wish they'd put my favorite comedian, _____
and her together. What a team they'd make!

She is _____, _____, and _____!
And I just love _____!

MY FAVORITE COMEDIAN

I think _____is the funniest
man in the whole world! The minute I see him on
_____ or in the _____, I start
to smile.

All he has to do is _____
and I am practically on the floor. When he _____
_____
_____
_____,
he is absolutely fabulous!

He's more than a funny man. He has a likable
personality, so that even when he's being serious,
I find myself _____
_____.

I also like him because he doesn't try to
hog the whole show. He'll share with _____
_____, or _____, or
whoever happens to be appearing with him. He
doesn't seem to mind if other people get laughs,
too.

He is _____ looking and _____! He is
also _____, _____, and he _____
well, too!

If you ever want a good laugh, be sure and catch
_____ whenever he appears!

WORLD'S WORST ACTRESS

_____ is the world's worst actress because she _____
_____
_____.

Her role in " _____ "
was _____. She played the part like
_____ and _____.
When I saw her in " _____ "
she continued to _____.
She can't _____, _____, or
_____! How she got where she is, I'll
never know. I think it's because she _____
_____.

Sometimes all it takes to become a big star is
_____ and _____!
Whatever happened to stars who could _____,
instead of just _____around and
_____!

I suppose there's an audience for that sort
of thing, but as for me, give me a star who can
_____, and not just _____!

WORLD'S WORST ACTOR

_____ is the world's worst
actor because _____
_____
_____.
  His movies have been _____.
When he gets a good role, he invariably _____
and _____ so much that you want to ____
_____.
  His television appearances have always been
_____ because
he _____ and _____ when he should
be _____ and _____.
  I saw him personally on the street and he
is _____, _____, and _____!
  What's more, he _____ when I asked him
for his autograph!
  I told him he could take it and _____ up
_____!
  He surprised me by _____!
You can _____ when you're a star, I suppose.

MY FAVORITE SINGER

(Male)

Every time I hear a _____
record, or see him on television, I have to stop
whatever I'm doing and _____.
When he sings I _____!
_____!
I feel like he's singing especially for _____!
The songs he records seem as if they were
written with _____
_____.
It's the kind of music people my age can identify
with, and surprisingly, Mom and Daddy think his
singing is _____!
I like the way he _____. Also
the way he _____, _____, and
_____! He seems equally at home
singing _____, _____, or
_____. He can perform all types
of songs with _____.
He's _____ and _____.
If I ever met him in person, I think I'd just
_____!

54

MY FAVORITE SINGER

(Female)

I love to watch _____ perform.
She has a _____ figure, and a _____ face,
and I like the way she wears her _____.
Add that to her _____ singing voice,
and you've got one of the _____
singers around. She's my favorite and she's __!
I enjoy all of her recordings, especially " _____
_____," "_____," and
"_____."

Her new album, called " _____,"
is really _____.
In it she sings _____,
_____,
_____,
and _____!

If I had to describe her voice, I'd say it was

_____.

I like her attitude, too. She acts as if _____

_____.

She has a _____ sense of humor and a
_____ personality. I admire her very much,
not only as a singer, but as _____

_____!

MY FAVORITE ROCK GROUP

_____ is my favorite rock
group. They are _____!
  When they hit the stage _____
_____
_____!
  Their costumes are _____! They come on
dressed like _____
_____
_____.
They are really "somethin' else!"
  They have their own special "sound." It's hard
to describe, but it's _____
_____!
All my friends love it!
  My parents think _____
_____.
  They have an album out called "_____
_____." In it you can hear such tunes as
"_____;" "_____
_____;" "_____,"
and "_____."
  If you like _____, then get
that album!

MY LEAST FAVORITE MUSICAL GROUP

_____ is my least favorite musical group. To even call them musical is _____.

Honestly, I don't see how _____
_____.

When they come on the stage, I _____
_____.

If I happen to hear a record of theirs on the radio I have to _____
_____.

The way they dress is _____
_____
_____.

Some of the songs they are offending our ears with are "_____" and
"_____, and I think _____!

I wish they'd _____
_____
_____!

If you like _____,
you'll love _____!

CHAPTER FOUR

SPECIAL DAYS

MY BIRTHDAY PARTY

My birthday party was _____
_____.
I am now _____ years old!
Many of my friends came to my party. _____,
_____, _____, _____, and
_____ were there. Others who came were
_____
We played games like _____,
_____, _____,
and _____.
They were very generous and brought me lots of
presents. I got _____, _____,
_____, _____, _____,
and _____and a lot of other
stuff!
I wasn't surprised when they brought out the
_____ cake and sang, "_____!"
But even though I was expecting it, I still felt thrilled
and embarrassed, all at the same time!
We had lots of goodies to eat, like _____,
_____, _____, and _____!
Everyone seemed to _____
and I can't wait until next year when I'm _____
years old. Maybe they'll _____again!

THE FOURTH OF JULY

The fourth of July means _____
_____
_____.
Most people celebrate the Fourth with _____
_____
and _____.
This July Fourth, my friends _____
and _____ and I went _____
_____.
There, we _____
_____.
We had _____and
_____ to eat.
Later, that night, we saw _____
_____
_____.

MY SUMMER VACATION

This summer I went to _____

_____

with _____.

  We had a _____ time,

The weather was _____ most

of the time. Other days were _____!

  I got to do a lot of _____,

_____, _____,

and _____.

  My favorite activity was _____

_____

  While on vacation, I met _____

_____

_____.

  Some of the sights I saw were _____,

_____, _____,

_____, and _____.

I brought back _____ for

_____ and _____

for _____.

  My vacation was _____

_____

and I hope _____

_____ next year.

60

THANKSGIVING DINNER

Thanksgiving is one of my favorite holidays. The delicious aroma of _____ fills our home. It is a day of warmth, good cheer, and _____.

What a feast we had! We ate _____, _____, _____, and _____.

I tried to save room for dessert, because we had _____. When I finished that, I was really _____!

It is nice that we set aside a day each year to _____.

I look forward to Thanksgiving because it makes me feel so _____!

Some of the friends and relatives who shared Thanksgiving with us were:

_____
_____
_____
_____
_____
_____

HALLOWEEN

This Halloween was _____!
I dressed as _____.
When I put on _____, I really
looked _____!
I think some of the younger kids were _____
when they saw me. The older kids _____
_____.

We all went trick-or-treating around the
neighborhood. Some of the people we spooked
were _____, _____, _____,
and _____. They all gave us lots
of goodies for our loot bags. I got _____,
_____, _____, _____,
_____, and _____.

I remembered not to accept any candy from
strangers, which is a very _____ rule
to follow.

This Halloween was _____
_____.
I am looking forward to next year, when I am going
to dress as _____ or _____!

THANKSGIVING DAY PARADE

My favorite float in the Thanksgiving Day Parade was _____.
It was _____ high and _____ wide.
I think it was _____
and when I saw it, I felt _____!
There were many different floats in the parade. All of them were _____.
Some of the more interesting ones were _____,
_____, _____,
_____, _____.
Of course, there were many marching bands, and I especially liked _____
and the _____.
My favorite clown was _____.
He did _____.
Santa Claus was the finale, and I _____
_____.
Parades are _____.
I think the Thanksgiving Day Parade is _____
_____!

CHRISTMAS

Christmas morning was _____!
I woke up at _____! When I arrived at the tree, I saw _____!
I was so excited! I could hardly wait to _____
_____. The first present I opened was _____.
It was from _____.
Some of the other presents I got were _____,
_____
_____
_____.
My favorite present was _____,
from _____.
I gave my parents _____
_____.
I gave my brother _____ and my sister _____.
Our pets got _____
_____.

It was a happy day for everyone, and one of the merriest Christmases ever!

MY NEW YEAR'S RESOLUTIONS

This year I made these resolutions. I resolve to:

_____
_____
_____
_____
_____
_____
_____
_____
_____
_____

Some people say New Year's resolutions are made to be broken, but I am going to try and keep all of mine!

CHAPTER FIVE

SPORTS REVIEW

MY FAVORITE SPORT

My favorite sport is _____.
I enjoy watching it on _____, but I'd
prefer going _____
and seeing the _____in person.
I think it is exciting when _____
_____
_____
_____really gets me going when there's
a _____.
Sometimes, when it's near the end of the game,
and the _____ have the _____
_____, I find myself sitting right on
the edge of my _____!
And when stars like _____and
_____ are playing, the tension
really mounts.
I like to play _____myself. I
play _____! I suppose if I
practice hard enough, I might be able to _____
_____ some day.
So whether I'm _____the game
on _____ or _____myself,
I think _____ is the _____
_____!

MY FAVORITE FOOTBALL PLAYER

My favorite football player is _____
_____. He plays _____
for the _____.
   I like him because he is _____
_____
_____.

   In one game I saw him _____
_____
_____
_____.

   In another game, he was _____
_____
_____.

   I always enjoy watching the _____
team play, because _____
_____.
   He does _____for
the team and is a _____sport, and
a _____ athlete.

MY FAVORITE BASEBALL PLAYER

My favorite baseball player is _____.
He plays _____ for the _____.
I like him because _____
_____
_____.
In one game he _____
_____!
In another game he _____
_____
His batting average is _____.
He has hit _____home runs. He is best known
for his _____.
Some of the outstanding things he has ac-
complished on the playing field are _____
_____
_____
_____
_____.
_____ is a real "pro," and I think
he's _____.

MY FAVORITE HOCKEY PLAYER

My favorite hockey player is _____.
He plays _____ for the _____.
I like him because _____
_____
_____.
In one game he _____
_____
_____.
In another game he _____
_____
_____.
He has got to be the best _____
in all of hockey. He can _____, _____,
and _____!
He is so _____!
He does _____for the
team and is a _____ athlete.

MY FAVORITE BASKETBALL PLAYER

My favorite basketball player is _____.
He plays _____ for the _____.
I like him because _____
_____
_____.
In one game he _____
_____
_____.
In another game he _____
_____
_____.
When he gets the ball _____
_____.
I love to watch him make _____ shots.
All in all, I think _____ is
the _____ in the game
of basketball.

MY FAVORITE TENNIS PLAYER

My favorite tennis player is _____.
(She/he) has won _____,
_____, and _____.
(She/he) has a good _____and
an excellent _____. (She/he) works
very hard and never seems to _____,
even when the going gets rough.
In one match _____
_____
_____.
In another match _____
_____
_____.
_____ is always exciting to
watch and I look forward to _____
_____
whenever I can.

THE NEWEST SPORT CRAZE
IN MY NEIGHBORHOOD

The newest sport craze in my neighborhood is
_____! It seems that every kid on my
block owns a _____. What makes
it so neat is the fact that you don't need much
equipment. All you need are _____, _____
and _____.

As far as clothes are concerned, you can simply
wear _____, _____ and _____.

Some of the kids like to _____while
they're _____, but I'm just learning how
to _____!

I think _____is fun for people of
all ages. However, my parents think _____
_____and whenever I ask them to try, they simply
say _____!

For my next birthday I hope I get _____
_____ so I can enjoy _____
even more!

CHAPTER SIX

LISTS

MY FAVORITE COMIC STRIPS

1. _____
2. _____
3. _____
4. _____
5. _____
6. _____
7. _____
8. _____
9. _____
10. _____

THE TEN GREATEST MOVIES!

You'll start feeling better right away after you've made this list! Think it over and list your ten all-time great movies!

1. _____
2. _____
3. _____
4. _____
5. _____
6. _____
7. _____
8. _____
9. _____
10. _____

THE TEN GREATEST NOVELS
EVER WRITTEN!

Another tough one! There are so many great ones!

1. _____
2. _____
3. _____
4. _____
5. _____
6. _____
7. _____
8. _____
9. _____
10. _____

MY FAVORITE CITIES
IN THE WHOLE WORLD!

If I had all the money I needed and could live *anywhere in the world*, I would have homes in these cities!

1. _____
2. _____
3. _____
4. _____
5. _____

MY FAVORITE CITIES
IN THE UNITED STATES!

Places I wouldn't mind living.

1. _____
2. _____
3. _____
4. _____
5. _____

REASONS

My reasons are: _____
_____
_____
_____
_____
_____
_____
_____
_____
_____
_____
_____
_____
_____

MY FIVE FAVORITE WOMEN IN HISTORY

1. _____
2. _____
3. _____
4. _____
5. _____

OTHERS

_____
_____
_____
_____
_____

COMMENTS

MY FIVE LEAST FAVORITE WOMEN
IN HISTORY

1. _____
2. _____
3. _____
4. _____
5. _____

OTHERS

_____
_____
_____
_____
_____

COMMENTS

MY FIVE FAVORITE MEN IN HISTORY

1. _____
2. _____
3. _____
4. _____
5. _____

OTHERS

_____
_____
_____
_____
_____

COMMENTS

MY FIVE LEAST FAVORITE MEN IN HISTORY

1. _____
2. _____
3. _____
4. _____
5. _____

OTHERS

_____
_____
_____
_____
_____

COMMENTS

CELEBRITIES I HAVE SEEN IN PERSON

_____
_____
_____
_____
_____
_____
_____
_____
_____

CELEBRITIES WHO GAVE ME
THEIR AUTOGRAPH

_____
_____
_____
_____

MY TEN FAVORITE RECORDING STARS!

1. _____
2. _____
3. _____
4. _____
5. _____
6. _____
7. _____
8. _____
9. _____
10. _____

COMMENTS

MY TEN ALL-TIME FAVORITE TV SHOWS!

1. _____
2. _____
3. _____
4. _____
5. _____
6. _____
7. _____
8. _____
9. _____
10. _____

GARY POOLE

A graduate of the American Academy of Dramatic Arts, Gary has appeared in some twenty-five plays. In radio he has worked as a disc jockey and talk show host. He spent seven years as the master of ceremonies for the Network Television Preview Theater in New York, testing pilot films in front of "live" audiences.

He is a former editor of *Golden Magazine* (Golden Press, New York), and has written stories for Rod Serling's "Twilight Zone," Boris Karloff's "Tales of Mystery," along with scripts for such cartoon characters as Bugs Bunny, Tweety and Sylvester, and Underdog. He wrote the comic book adaptation of the 1977 version of *King Kong,* and is the author of a book on Donny and Marie Osmond. He also wrote the novelization of the Walt Disney movie, *The Apple Dumpling Gang Rides Again,* and is the author of *TV Comedians*.

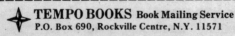